Authors:
Joshua De Sousa
Kimberly Stratton

Publisher: The Crown And Cross
Consulting And Publishing Co LLC

Cover: Joshua De Sousa

Originally printed in the United States of America

The Crown And Cross Consulting And Publishing Co LLC
Attention: Kimberly Stratton
PO Box 952607
Lake Mary, FL 32795

ISBN: 979-8-9853754-6-6

Intentionally blank page

Dedication Page

Thank You, Lord, for creating me, loving me and showing me how to fly in your freedom.

Thank you to my parents, grandparents and family for all the love and support.

Thank you to all my friends, chosen brothers and sisters and spiritual family who ensured that I always knew my worth.

Thank you to Pastor Angel Holcomb, Prophetess Jerri Robinson, Pastor Tamara Bethea, Prophetess Monique Rodgers and Pastor Kimberly Stratton for being some of the greatest influences in my life. I would have not been able to soar without any of you!

Signed,

Joshua De Sousa

Dedication Page

I thank God for this opportunity. In this season of my life, I want to be so obedient to Him that it is like breathing – it just happens automatically without thought, doubt, insecurities or interference of any kind. Secondly, I thank God for my Mom Patricia Marine and my Dad Teddy Price. Their words of encouragement rang in my ears and helped fuel me on those 2am writings that I was determined (yet so tired) but I knew had to be completed. Next, I want to thank Joshua for his obedience in collaborating on this project. I am so grateful for this season – however long – that God allows our paths to continue to cross. You are truly a blessing Man of God. Last but certainly not least, I want to thank all my family (*blood and not by blood*), friends, loved ones, Mothers of Wisdom and of Zion, *Church At The Well* Leadership (including Saints, members and friends of CATW) as well as those spiritual warriors including all authors/supporters of *The Crown And Cross Consulting And Publishing Co LLC* for all of their prayers, laughter, genuine support and heartfelt love.

Signed,

Kimberly Stratton

Table of Contents

Table of Contents cont'd

Prologue

With all that we have suffered through in life and on our journey with Christ, we have been through a process. We, just like the butterfly, transform from the "ugly" caterpillar stage (which is still beautiful in God's eyes) into a beautiful work of art; still able to be utilized. We all go through a process and eventually evolve – like the stages a butterfly goes through – to then blossom into this amazing vessel fit for the Master's use and glory. As the butterfly is released from its last stage, just as God releases us into the world, we spread our wings telling any and everyone our testimony which entails the goodness of God and spreading the Good News that includes freedom in Christ. For we are not bitter for what we went through and are no longer broken but instead blessed.

We pray that as you read the pages of our individual experiences in this unified collaboration, you are not only captured by our personal yet synchronized journeys but that you too can relate.

Signed,

Joshua De Sousa and Kimberly Stratton

THE BUTTERFLY EVOLUTION - DE SOUSA AND STRATTON
The Butterfly Evolution
From Broken to Blessed
Joshua De Sousa + Kimberly Stratton

Intentionally blank page

Joshua De Sousa
Author, Minister,
Youth Leader, Ghostwriter,
Writing Coach, Founder of
Sousa Scribal Solutions, LLC
and the Supernatural Scribes
Writing Conference

The Egg Stage

Chapter 1

The Broken Egg

So many characters I watched on television and at movie theaters have some sort of tragic birth story. Many characters lose their parents or guardians upon birth or shortly after. Others become orphans and never find out who their parents are and then some are old enough to witness the moment of loss that shapes their mentality and emotions. Other characters in pop culture, have some tragic accidents that permanently damage them forever such as figuring out how to overcome despite a disability or birth defect. They would be oblivious to it until later in life, where their differences made it hard for them to fit in and find friendship or companionship. However, just because an egg is broken or compromised does not mean it cannot birth greatness.

Two scenarios stick out because of how much they resonate with me. The first one I want to bring up is the story of two fish who had hundreds of eggs and named them all with much excitement. They were looking forward to the eventual arrival of their precious children, until out of nowhere, an even bigger fish who was like a monster to them came and attacked them.

The father fish was knocked unconscious, waking up to his wife and all their eggs completely gone. The monster fish ate all of them and left this father all alone and broken. However, as he was weeping, he saw one fish remained whose eggshell was cracked. The father held tightly to this fish and called him Nemo, whose cracked shell ended up limiting his mobility due to one of his fins ended up deformed and small compared to his other one.

As Nemo got older, it was apparent that he could only use one of his "hands," but he and his father would call the deformed one a "lucky fin." They tried not to look at what Nemo lacked as a curse but more so as evidence that he survived when he should have died. It was worn as a battle scar; surviving the wrath of the monster that took their entire family away from them. Of course, this would cause the father to be overprotective of him, as Nemo's carelessness and desire for independence led to his being kidnapped by humans. However, as this father and son traveled far and wide across the sea and land to find each other, they had to remember that if they survived the brokenness of the past, they would be able to reunite and realize they are stronger than they ever could imagine.

Another example I would like to share follows the tale of a tribe of penguins, who were all strangely gifted with singing, as if it was part of their genetics. It was a requirement that all of them found a genre of music to specialize in and they were conditioned to fall in love based on their ability to win hearts over with their vocals. Two penguins fell in love as they sang to each other and it resulted in an egg. The father carried this egg in the harsh cold to keep it nice and warm but somehow, he dropped the egg and it fell into the cold snow. Just those few moments away from a parent's warmth could cause a deformity. When the child named Mumble grew up, he not only looked different from the rest of the penguins but he was unable to sing.

He failed all his singing classes and no one in the penguin village would accept him but he instead developed a special gift for tap dancing, which was a side effect of his compromised birthing process. Everyone hated him for his uniqueness but when they were facing the threat of famine, it would be his tapping that entertained humans who were able to provide fish for them all and save them from starvation. It honestly was not until recently that I realized how much the movies *Finding Nemo* and *Happy Feet* parallel my own journey, for I too survived being born in a broken egg. When you are in an egg or a placenta, if you are being born by a mammal or human, you are soft and defenseless needing only one wrong shove, one bad drink, use of one drug or one sickness to completely destroy you. So many scenarios that my parents endured attempted to break my egg but I am alive and able to tell how the weapons formed against me did not prosper.

Just as Nemo was the only egg left, my parents tried over and over again to have children for nearly a decade with no evidence of conception. Parenting seemed quite hopeless until my mother finally became pregnant in 1996. However, life became quite difficult for both of them during my egg season. My father lost his job and had a hard time finding another, forcing my mom to be the sole financial resource while expecting me. This caused a lot of anger, strife, frustration and bitterness, which is not good for your blood pressure or for the baby's health. Negative emotions like these can cause strokes, heart attacks and jaundice. After a long 12-hour labor on

November 5th, I came out of my mother's womb covered with the yellow skin that jaundice produces due to the difficult journey leading up to my arrival.

That was only the beginning of the many sorrows I would face during my journey as a broken egg. In the same way I was initially covered in a disease that represents anger and strife. I dealt with so much hate, rejection, envy and bitterness from those whom I loved and wanted to be loved by. I felt like a black sheep everywhere I went: school, church and even wanting to be cherished by many of my family members, specifically the cousins on my dad's side. However, I am here to let you know that just like Mumble and Nemo, I found my way through all the brokenness, poverty, failure, depression and insecurity that attempted to destroy my destiny. As you read the following pages, you will see how the Lord allowed me to flourish and eventually fly in a faith that could not be taken away from me.

The Larva Stage

Chapter 2

The Caterpillar's Cultivation

Growing up was pretty average for me as I was oblivious to a lot that went on around me during my formative years. I was dedicated a few months after birth (which basically meant a pastor or priest said a special prayer to God and asked Him to protect and guide you during the course of your life). I vividly remember that sanctuary since we spent the first five years of my life there. Even before I officially declared that I believed in God, I was always attracted to the church and drawn by all its aspects. The soul-stirring music, unique building structures, those ginormous crosses behind the pulpit and the sun's reflection through the stained-glass windows all left deep impressions on my being just like a tattoo. Even when I was in the car with my parents and grandparents, I always stared outside in awe whenever we passed by a church, wanting to visit every single one I could.

There was a season when we did not go to church at all but as I became older, I transitioned and attended church Monday through Friday. From kindergarten all the way to middle school, I was enrolled in private Christian schools that instilled prayer and we studied the Bible daily. Honestly, I was what you would call a "part-time honor roll student", for my grades could waver between A and C quarter to quarter. However, the two classes I would always do my best in were English and Bible. Bible was my favorite subject each year, enjoying all the pictures of the stories and being able to watch movies about the events as well. We had chapel services every Wednesday, singing songs that I still hear in many worship services today. All this immersion of information about an invisible man gave me the courage to embrace Him as my personal God and Lord, declaring myself a believer at 8 years old in my classroom.

I thoroughly enjoyed this faith that I accepted. It was and still is a huge part of who I am. If I was a caterpillar, I believe this would take up at least half of the legs on my body that helped me navigate my life. My whole identity was based on who I believed in, especially because I grew to despise my appearance as a caterpillar. In addition to being one of the shortest kids in all my classrooms, I was also one of the largest in weight. One of my lifelong limits and deformities has been my weight and my asthma, for being unable to breathe made it increasingly difficult to work out in order to lose weight. The result unfortunately would be more and more pounds added onto me as the years went by. Between this and having a very soft and gentle demeanor, I was the recipient of much ridicule and rejection.

I despised gym classes and strenuous activities at summer camp because my limits were fully on display. I would cost the team points because I was too slow to finish the race or to catch the ball. I was so afraid of heights and other activities that the teachers would have to stop everything when I started crying and freaking out. When someone insulted me, I would not even try to hit them because I knew I was weak. I would immediately revert to tears, a behavior that lasted all the way until 8th grade. Even as I began to develop crushes on some of the girls at my school, I would lose it when other kids told them I liked them. I already knew they were never going to like me back, which they did not.

I always struggled with confidence and self-esteem and I would dread the insults waiting for me every day. However, God looked out for me and defended me. Even though I was unable or willing to fight when people teased me, other classmates would come to my defense. It was not until I got a little older that I began to make male friends because most of the guys wanted nothing to do with me. By the time I got to 5th Grade, some of the older kids from 6th and 7th Grade would look out for me and always let me sit with them, hang out with them and told me they would confront anyone who was bothering me. It was these things that caused me to look up towards the sun or should I say the Son. Promises of His love and presence kept me through all the distractions and attacks on my heart.

Even as I crawled on my back, feeling slow and shameful, I knew I was loved and appreciated. Even though I was not the best student, I knew I was wise and intelligent. I had no clue what my purpose was yet but I did figure out that one of my greatest strengths was showing kindness to people who tried to kill my confidence and joy. Apparently, I was so kind that I won several awards at my middle school each year for being the most Christlike child in my class. That was enough for me to see that despite everything I seemingly lacked, I still had much to offer. I would be the one who others can talk to for a laugh, a kind word, or even a prayer. By the time graduation rolled around, even those who bullied me had no choice but to respect me, especially when they saw on the graduation program what my dream was for my future.

I spent my entire childhood trying to survive school, hating myself but learning so much about myself at the same time. I continued to keep myself nourished by the fruit of my faith, cherishing every moment in His presence and celebrating every time I successfully memorized a scripture. Even though people did not hang out with me or rarely invited me to their sleepovers and parties, I was okay with it because I was being sustained by a love greater than anything in this world. It was made known to me that people harmed others due to their own insecurities and the issues of life they had to go home to, so the least I could do was pray for them after I finished crying about the insults hurled at me.

Between my Bible, my favorite movies and my favorite video games, I was able to find safety and paradise. All those hobbies including swimming, spending time with my grandparents and eventually going back to church for myself when I was 12, all were the legs I leaned on to navigate my journey as an outsider. Even though I was not good at many things, this would help me narrow down what my true purpose consisted of. If you are not careful, you will allow people to limit you to what is seen presently when you are just a caterpillar. All the words, insults, judgments and negative opinions you hear now will be temporary. As you grow older, you are going to forget the majority of the times you cried and questioned your worth. One thing that will surely help you is looking around and seeing that your crawling season is only temporary because you see others who are soaring that you can literally look up to.

Chapter 3

The Higher Call

I wonder what the caterpillar does during the first stage of its life as it functions the way it was created to. They become complacent and comfortable with their daily routine of crawling, eating leaves and fruit and repeating it without a care in the world. However, I have always been curious. If something happens within their mind when they see someone or something that looks familiar and foreign at the same time. What happens when a caterpillar is crawling around and sees a creature with orange wings fly past them? Is there an instinct or spark of inspiration that lets them know there is more in store for them? While I cannot answer on behalf of a caterpillar, I can answer for my own life. Truly, watching the butterflies in my life helped me understand that my caterpillar days would eventually come to an end.

As I mentioned before, I made the decision to go back to church for myself in 2009 at the age of 12. I pushed my parents into making the effort of waking up early on Sunday mornings and visiting a church that we went to a few times a year. I eagerly walked down the aisle to join the church after attending for a whole month and I was baptized that May. From that moment on, my instincts began to awaken. My foundation that was already set by attending Christian school started to make sense, and the more I served, the more my soul longed for a deeper purpose. Until that season, I had no idea what I wanted to do with my life. By the first quarter of 2010, I let my parents know that I came to an understanding that I never imagined to be my reality.

The following sentence would come out of my mouth: "I think I am supposed to be a preacher." There was silence for ten seconds as my parents processed this confession because when my father was younger, ministry was a desire of his as well. However, due to the issues of life and becoming derailed from destiny, he never pursued it and I watched him looking aimlessly for his purpose outside of obedience. My confession was a conviction for him, for it was as if God used me to shake him up and realize that He still needs him to walk in this as well. I know most people say that when God calls them to ministry, they run and rebel against Him. That was not me. I was eager and excited and truly desired to carry out this assignment even as a teenager.

I told everyone at school and everyone at church that I finally found my dream and I began to study other preachers, both old and young. I was deeply inspired by all the preachers I saw on television, and then by preachers in their teens and twenties on YouTube who were already traveling across the world. It seemed so impossible to me but I prayed for the same to happen to me. Because I was bold enough to believe in myself, others in the church believed in me and recommended me for leadership conferences and preaching opportunities. I would receive my very first invitation to preach for five minutes at a youth service in Newark, New Jersey in 2011. I had no idea what I was doing but I kept getting invited back and one door led to another. By my third preaching opportunity in October 2011, I was able to minister at a youth conference for one of the bishops of the denomination I was under at the time.

When other pastors saw my videos online, they asked me to minister for their youth services and youth conferences. I was preaching at least once a quarter or sometimes even once a month. There was this rush of fulfillment that I could not explain every time I mounted a pulpit, finding out that there was a higher call on my life. I went from watching other men and women do this thing to now being considered amongst them and preaching alongside the local pastors that I looked up to. From that moment on, God surrounded this caterpillar with butterflies. He gave me mentors and role models whom I did not have to watch on a screen but who took the time to train me, pour into me and recommend me for even more chances to spread the word of God all around my state.

However, one thing I would learn early on in my development is that some butterflies will be threatened by a caterpillar's potential, fearing that they will shine brighter than them once they become fully aware of who they are. Even though many pastors rallied around me and supported my emergence as a caterpillar, there was one butterfly who I wished affirmed and noticed me. My very own pastor was my newest bully, whose words hurt more than any of the times I was called fat or ugly by classmates in middle and high school. He would always mock and shut down my confession of desiring to walk in ministry. There was even an instance when he told me to write a paper explaining my calling, having it due in May 2012 but not reading it until December 2012 while saying it was a waste of his time.

The biggest war I had to fight was every time I saw his face, preparing for him like I did the boys at school who would either insult me, throw school supplies and balls at me and even slap or squeeze me inappropriately because they said I had the body parts of a woman. Every ministry I would try to serve on, my pastor would always make excuses as to why I could not serve in that capacity and would sometimes mysteriously shut it down or cancel their operations entirely. Every time I asked him for permission to accept my preaching invitations, he would say that I could go if I remembered that I would never be a true preacher and that he will never certify me or let me touch his pulpit.

Despite all these things, there was an unshakeable resolve inside of me. I preached through the depression that began to overtake me, the many tears I cried after his verbal abuse sessions in his church office and the insecurities of not knowing if I would ever be considered legitimate. I continued to lift my head to the sky, where I would see the other butterflies that God already allowed to flourish and walk in His favor. I had to believe Him for the impossible, knowing that one way or another, I would be able to fly among the others without fear or restraint. I held on to the hope that there were wings inside of me that would continue to be developed as I crawled through my daily routine.

Chapter 4

Crawling with Broken Legs

High school and church felt like I was between a rock and a hard place as I struggled with my identity and limitations. Everyone wanted me to be something I could never be and the man I trusted to help me kept me away from the one thing I desired to be the most. My high school was a non-negotiable decision from my family. They had an unreasonable overemphasis on sports, making people like me feel inferior because I was too physically unfit to play any of them. Not a day would go by when other students told me join a sport, lose weight or maybe stay in the bathroom for two hours and push the weight out of my stomach. I was greatly insulted for participating in “soft activities” such as choir and theater because they were looked down on.

It did not matter that I was doing work for the church outside of school, for they only cared about what you did after hours on campus. I did serve as one of the managers for the fencing team but that was one of my worst experiences ever. My grades reached an all-time low because of how drained I was between the fencing coach cursing me out for not knowing what I was doing and even insulting my faith frequently. I despised high school and I felt like no matter how hard I was trying to please God, I could not please anyone else. My insecurities grew larger and I had a hard time talking to girls since there was not enough interaction with them. By my junior and senior years, I was waiting for our school prom. Not only did we not have one but no girl I knew asked me to their prom either.

Every time I tried to tell someone I liked that I had feelings for them, it would either end with all their friends laughing at me or them staying away from me entirely. My confidence was stolen from me in every single way imaginable and all I had left to hold on to was my dreams and my faith. So many people counted me out back during freshman year when we had to complete a mandatory hike as a rite of passage to move on to the next grade. No one wanted me on their team and I was stuck with the outcasts whom no one wanted either. We were the very last to finish the hike but I did not care because it was not a race. It was proof to me that I could continue to crawl with courage no matter what I faced because my best friend said if I were to quit on the hike so easily, then imagine what I would do if the weight of ministry became difficult.

Mind you, he said this in 2011 before my pastor started becoming verbally abusive so that surely was a prophetic unction. It is a miracle that I did not drop out of high school or walk away from church during this formative season. I persevered through all the persecution and leaned on God's strength despite my limitations. I saw a way out of my torment by going to a Christian college in a different state, for I believed that another church would gladly hire and train me after receiving a bible degree in either theology or youth ministry. When I got to the beautiful campus of Eastern University in August of 2014, I thought it would be the perfect place to spend my last stage as a caterpillar. At first glance, it felt like the paradise I always desired.

It felt so good to no longer wear a school uniform, for sports to no longer be mandatory and of course to finally be around women again. One of the last parts of my caterpillar season was finalizing what I wanted to be and deciding to be fearless about my career path. Youth ministry and pastoring in general was my deepest desire and I saw no room for any other degree or practice outside of it since I was not good at any other topic either. Many in my family and my church begged me to study something that I could get some real money with but I had to be okay with not living up to people's expectations anymore. When I came to this conclusion, a special opportunity awaited me.

I pushed past my insecurities as a preacher to apply for the college's campus ministry, which was called the Student Chaplaincy, where we would be in charge of hosting bible studies in our dormitory apartments and be available as spiritual advisors for our classmates. There was a warm sense of healing and affirmation when I was told that I was chosen to be one of the student chaplains for the following school year. I will not lie when I say I began to laugh at my pastor in my mind, for yet another group of people whom I just met also saw the calling he was too blind and prideful to see. I spent every day afterward quoting a line from Trip Lee's song *One Sixteen*, "I ain't got no white collar; He (God) made me a priest though." It honestly felt like it was the ordination I spent my entire adolescence waiting for.

I still wrestled with the fact that I felt like I lost so much during my childhood and adolescence due to the consecrated life I chose to live. There were times when even youth pastors and other church kids I knew said I was too holy and too deep, even though I could not help that my advanced spiritual maturity came through the Holy Spirit. At least now as a student chaplain, I can use all the sermons and teachings I have been working on in private for years, believing that my choice to pursue my calling at a young age was not in vain. God surrounded me with a tribe of believers and fellow preachers in college who also felt led to walk into the ministry but because I did not cherish them trying to chase other people, I became more broken than I ever was before.

In my pursuit of chasing butterflies, I ended up distracted by moths, who appear to be flying but are truly dull and lack God's glory. I chased this woman who I thought was perfect but what was perceived as perfection was only skin deep. She hung out with the wrong crowd and I wanted to be accepted by her peers so badly. Unfortunately, the enemy took my desire for love and used it to destroy me, breaking my legs and mobility as a caterpillar. I cannot move anymore. I cannot breathe anymore. I cannot pray anymore. I cannot study anymore. I did not lose my will to live but I lost the ability to function. My heart was in so much pain and it seemed like I could not get enough sleep. I hid my suffering as much as I could from my friends and family but it would only last until my inability to function in class resulted in me failing too many times by December 2016 and being told I could not come back. This was the beginning of the end of Joshua as I knew him.

The Pupa/Chrysalis "transition" Stage

Chapter 5

Suffocated by Suffering

There comes a time in the caterpillar's life when he or she has no other choice but to die. Their bodies feel completely out of sorts and they have a deeper awareness that life as they knew it has come to an end. They must surrender to the process of their biology and embrace that the only way to be reborn is to be buried. At that moment, they find an area to crawl up to one last time, hang from that seemingly final resting place and close their eyes as a deep sleep comes over them. The chrysalis begins to form around them, encasing them with no room to breathe or move, causing the death of the old life and the start of the new one. In the same manner, God will call you to a higher place but it will not be without you having to watch the old version of you die in the process. He will break your legs until you have no other choice but to surrender to the process and be still enough to begin the rebirth. When you are done, you will not need all those old legs and dead weight.

I need to backtrack and let you know that my countdown to the coffin (called a chrysalis) started the minute I ran to my room and cried in the fall of 2015 after the beautiful moth I wanted to be with said I took all her kindness and words the wrong way. Even though the Lord showed me the truth about her being ashamed due to how her friends believed that she was settling, it did not change the fact that her cold shoulder felt like an icicle piercing my heart. She was both Judas and Peter at the same time, betraying me with kind words, hugs and hints of interest, only to take it all back and swear that she never knew me. I thought I was going to college but instead, God enrolled me in the school of suffering.

I do not believe God wanted this to happen to me because I can truly admit that it was my fault that I got distracted by my feelings and did not focus as I should have. I was so disheveled from my long history of rejection, that if the spirit of rejection was cancer, this would have taken me to stage four. Even though I fell for the enemy's trap and allowed a moth to interfere with my metamorphosis, the Lord still found a way to make this work for my good. This suffering made me cry out to God from the depths of my soul. My prophetic gifts and discernment became sharper than ever, being able to understand behind the scenes why I was suffering in every single area of my life. For the first time ever to my knowledge,

God visited me in the middle of the night and called my name in a soft but strong whisper until I answered Him.

When I heard His voice loud and clear in April 2016, I woke up from that encounter with such peace and joy. I had no idea that it was possible to be so depressed and broken; yet, so hopeful and joyful at the same time. Even though I was going through so much agony, I had this undeniable feeling that everything was going to be okay. If I was removed from college in the next few months, God was going to take care of me. Even though I really wanted this girl, God would one day allow me to believe in love again. Even if I ended up stuck in New Jersey, God would make a way for me to still grow in ministry. The same way Jesus submitted to death on a cross, I submitted to the chrysalis that I had to use the last of my strength to walk into and allow myself to be concealed into.

My pain and peace coexisted within me as I walked through a door that I thought would finally change my life. Despite my failures and immense hardship, I was invited by one of the many pastors I trusted to finally be trained and certified as a preacher under them. They needed a youth pastor and said I would be perfect for it, especially because they did not want me wasting away under the pastor who swore he was never going to let me become the real deal. 2017 started with me crying every Sunday at church, many thinking it was worship when in reality it was sorrow. Honestly, it was both because I knew if I gave God my tears, He would evaporate them and use them as rain to water the seeds of my harvest. I knew He would make a testimony out of my test but I had no clue that it could get even worse than it already was.

Verbal abuse is not just talking down on someone but it is smooth-talking them with manipulation and making them dependent on your words, especially when they prey on your insecurities. My new pastor started to show all these red flags in his conversations with me and I kept trying to ignore them. By this time, I had already waited 7 long years to be licensed as a minister and I knew no man was perfect; however, he began to put me in compromising situations that went against the fullness of my purpose. He knew I had no money but he complained about my lack of dress clothes. He never announced online when it was my turn to preach but always celebrated other young guest preachers more than me,

whispering in my ear to take notes on how to dress and preach like them so I could get the same doors they do.
By the summer of 2017, he was blatant about his disdain towards my beliefs about the other expressions of Christianity that he and the group of churches he was under did not believe in. He told me I was bipolar and double-minded in my theology because I was trying too hard to be Baptist and Pentecostal at the same time. Last time I checked, the prophetic and spiritual gifts are not a denomination. He wanted me to think about whether I truly wanted to be a Baptist minister or not and I silently already knew my decision. I would not comply. God continued to allow other prophets to speak life into me. They confirmed that in this temporary coffin that I found myself in, I would find my wings and my true identity as a prophet. I did not know what was going to happen but since I was already dead and numb to the pain, I could handle a few more hits.

By the end of 2017, the pastor said he was delaying my licensing ceremony until I complied with several of his requests such as I needed to get some money and dress up more, I needed to please his friends and peers with my preaching and appearance and ultimately, I could not openly profess that I believed in the prophetic. He told me I needed to cut off anyone who was filling my head with junk and that he cannot have me making him look bad. One meeting later, he saw how frustrated I became with him, and he would attempt to lie on God's name, saying God would close my mouth and never let me preach again a day in my life if I did not submit to his demands and tried to leave. A few days later, I left, letting him know that his vision for me and God's vision for me were two completely different things.

Now, that was two horrible Decembers in a row in 2016 and 2017, where I literally lost everything that I ever wanted. The potential of finally being an official preacher kept me from going insane after all the sorrow I faced at college and all the years before it. The isolation and loneliness of my chrysalis began to truly set in, as when I left my second pastor, my name was destroyed beyond repair amongst many people in New Jersey. Many of those who I looked up to as butterflies all turned out to be moths with dull discernment and a lack of glory and individuality. They were too busy trying to impress each other and compete with one another at the expense of other people's hearts. So many people wanted nothing more to do with me anymore and I had no idea that I was about to go into a season where I would not preach at all for quite some time. With no job, no degree and no ministry, I was forced to lie still in the chrysalis of cultivation.

Chapter 6

Evidence of Emergence

This chrysalis is cold and I am stuck with nothing but my failures and frustration. Why did God let this happen to me? Why did He leave me here? Why is this necessary in order to become everything He promised I would be? These were all the questions I asked when I was hidden and hopeless. There was no one I could turn to, so I had no choice but to make my post at a beautiful, large, Pentecostal church thirty minutes away from me. This place kept me alive and the worship was exciting. Initially, I was starstruck that all my favorite famous preachers came here. It was surely an experience being able to witness these butterflies in their element up close and personal, reminding me that someday, maybe I can still fly too.

There is still an issue with this beautiful cave. Sadly, it became a gift graveyard. I grew in the presence of God because the pastor and famous guest preachers preached about everything I believed in. We believed in the prophetic, miracles, the fivefold and much more but it was all talk and no action. We just got to sit back and watch those on the pulpit show off their gifts but I was surrounded by unveiled cocoons. Even though I was content with serving here, it would not be long before I felt hopelessness regarding ministry. I have no clue why God sent me here when clearly no one is allowed to fly here. They are just forced to cater to the leader from their permanently sealed cocoon.

In the midst of all of this, my best friend took me on his back like the Good Samaritan did for the man bleeding and broken on the street. We went to various conferences and services where we were able to watch newly emerged butterflies walk in their purpose and teach others how to do the same. Many generals and trailblazers also came to us while we sat in the pew and reminded us of the potency of our purpose, telling me not to give up and to remember who I am. They boldly called me a prophet and said they do not care who tried to tell me otherwise. I had to believe in myself again and allow the transformation to happen privately in this cocoon before my Lord puts me on display.

In addition, a woman who I met at a former mentor's preaching conference truly picked me up in the darkest of times. She called me and asked me if I can come and pray for her prayer line once a month. I agreed because it was not like I had anything else to do. I was going to crawl right back in my bed of sadness as soon as I was done, since I did not have a job or ministry to attend. For the next few years of my life, my favorite day of the month became the first Monday because each time I taught on the prayer line was a reminder that Joshua was (and still is) there. It was evident that I still had something to contribute to the body of Christ. Giving those fifteen-minute messages and prayers and receiving a text message from her afterward on how powerful the tubes in my spiritual hospital bed were, as I endured this coma.

In September 2018, my best friend and I went on one of our many church adventures that helped us transition from our traditional background so that we could fully embrace who we were in Christ. This led us all the way to Baltimore, Maryland where a prayer conference shifted us like never before. During that weekend, I found the evidence I was looking for. I knew I could preach but I had no idea that I could walk in the supernatural. This was the moment that I realized the cocoon was doing its job and that I was a caterpillar no more. God used me to lay hands on my best friend's back and declare healing over his spine and when we were done praying, he said he stood up straight for the first time ever in his life. In the midst of my darkness, I discovered destiny. I was walking in the deeper things of God that people tried to keep me away from.

The cave, coma, coffin and cocoon that I was in was not the most comfortable but I am grateful that I felt the warmth of God's hand. I still had no clue how I was going to emerge or who was going to help me. I tried my best not to worry about it and realized that God will call me to the forefront with or without the help of others. He does not need moths trying to teach me how to become a butterfly. I could not afford to lose sight of my purpose as a butterfly by feeling inadequate and inferior to moths. I dared not get distracted by platforms, popularity, big followings and the ability to wow and entertain the crowd. God kept moths away from me so that they would not prematurely open my cocoon for me so that they could take credit for my current season.

Chapter 7

I Am Not Isolated, I Am Consecrated

I wish my eyes were closed while evolving and emerging so that I would not be comparing myself to others who were flying around me. I became everyone's biggest supporter while I was stuck in a prolonged process. I watched everyone graduate college ahead of me, get jobs before me and become ministers, prophets, youth pastors and even lead pastors before me. Even though I understood the season I was in and that I could not just have any old job or be ordained in any old church, it still felt unfair to me. I know I was not perfect but I felt like I was so faithful and loyal to so many people, not deserving to be treated so poorly by everyone who abandoned and abused me.

When you are evolving in that shell, this is the season where God allows you to shed that dead weight. All those legs you needed before, you only need a few now. You must rest in Him just a little longer and it is eventually all going to make sense. By 2019, I had to remind myself that I had one hope left. I did not have anything that society says a man is supposed to have by now, but all I had left was a pen. I knew God called me to be a writer and an author because many preachers commented on how excellent my sermons were a few years back. I had no idea how to get in this field but I started searching for resources that would help me break free and find my own path. I decided that even if I never touched a pulpit ever again, I was still going to preach the gospel with my pen.

I went to a writing conference by faith and I mean the whole process was by faith. I had no money at all and had to ask so many friends, church members and family members for help to get there. I had to let them know I was on the verge of finally finding out what my wings were made of and I needed help to understand what I was getting into. Within a matter of days, I received more than enough to register for the conference and travel to and from. I gleaned so much from all these writers who spoke and taught. There was one in particular who pulled me to the side and said she could tell I was a prophetic writer and gave me a $50 dollar bill stating that I have walked into a season of jubilee. From that day onward, I picked up my pen and wrote like my life depended on it.

I always made powerful posts on social media but I began to create blog posts that I knew those who consistently supported me could read. One of my favorite blog posts back then was called "The Butterfly Breakthrough", where I talked about how a butterfly is always there inside of the caterpillar the entire time. I stated how God knew our whole purpose and identity before we were ever aware. Even Jesus Himself, the Son of God, had to go through a rediscovery process. He spent His entire childhood and young adulthood discovering His assignment as the chosen Messiah so that He would fully know who He was by his thirties. When it was time for Him to walk in the fullness of His assignment, He had to be ready to die, for it was the only way for Him to walk in resurrection and eternal life.

When I embraced my assignment not just as a preacher but also as a writer, I had to be prepared for the celebration that would turn into criticism. I had to be prepared for people who would be threatened by the fact that I was "preaching in a book without a title." The Lord used every storm I endured to give me enough tough skin to handle the rejection and attacks to come because my purpose as a writer was more than just my own books. I had no clue that writing an email devotional every month was going to thrust me into leadership. Just within two months of writing free devotionals, I ministered to over 200 people across the world from the United States, Africa, the Caribbean Islands and Europe. My pen took my ministry higher than ever before and I began to see the first tear in my cocoon, seeing that the season of emergence was slowly but surely coming upon me.

The Adult Stage

Chapter 8

The Wind Beneath My Wings

God made it so that when the butterfly has fully become what it was always meant to be, there is one last thing it has to do to confirm that it is truly ready for the next level. When the cocoon is formed, it takes 10 to 14 days for the caterpillar to "die" and become reborn as the butterfly that was encrypted in its DNA. The chrysalis is initially solid and firm but when the time is right, it becomes soft and transparent; allowing all to see that at any moment, this butterfly is about to break free and soar to new heights. However, during that day of emergence, there are two types of battles the butterfly must face: the battle within of having to push itself out to prove it is strong enough and the battle around people or other creatures spectating and hoping it does not survive.

When I went silent and my ministry was seemingly dead in the eyes of many, the Lord purposely made my cocoon solid and impenetrable so that no one could see through it. I missed the visibility I had growing up as well as all the potential doors and connections waiting for me through the people I was around at that time. However, that was not His plan for me. He showed me as I matured that I was thinking way too small. I was reducing His power and my creativity to a microphone, when that is an insult to all He has placed inside of me. I was like the man with the money in Matthew 25 that was ironically called "talents," trying too hard to hide what I have because I thought so little of it. Preaching was not the fullness of my assignment but rather the root of all the fruit that was about to spring forth.

God showed me that He was not punishing me when He allowed all those complacent caterpillars and malicious moths to leave me be. They thought if they sealed me and glued my cocoon shut by telling others to stay away from me, I would die and be forgotten. However, they failed to realize that butterflies are not actually supposed to have help breaking free from their chrysalis. If you tear it open for them, they will fall to the ground and wither away. The final test is for them to be able to push themselves out of the womb they encased themselves in. This is the only way to put their new bodies to the test, developing the strength and stamina to handle the weight of their wings, and the wind they will have to fly through for the rest of their lives.

For many of you, you may not yet realize that you are no longer a caterpillar. You have been in the darkness for so long that you forgot about the light; however, you must remember that Christ's light can shine inside of you even when there is no light around you. Allow him to light up your cocoon before it becomes clear and permeable by sunlight, so that you can see you are a new creature. You already have been healed, delivered and transformed but you must now exercise your freedom. It is your responsibility to use your authority to break yourself out of the shell, so that you are strong enough to carry your own weight. There will be turbulence and rainy days, so you must master bursting out your comfort zone so that you will not collapse when confusion comes.

In 2020, I honestly did not believe I was transformed yet. I still felt inferior and insecure to everyone else around me and I could not see the light even though I held on to the faint hope that my pen began to provide. Not even two weeks into the new year, I received a phone call that changed my entire life. A lady called me who I was friends with but have not heard from in a while. She told me immediately that the Lord had been telling her to talk to me for over three months about a special need. She was trying to write her book for quite some time, advertising the cover for over two years. She kept wanting to give up because of all the backlash, resistance, and sabotage from those she trusted. Apparently, the Lord told her to try one more time by asking me to type it up for her.

My response was that of someone who did not realize they were ready to come out of hiding. I gave all these excuses just like Moses did when God appeared to him in a burning bush in Exodus 3. God was calling me higher and I tried to deny and denounce that I was ready or worthy. I told her it makes no sense because I failed school, people critiqued my lackluster writing skills when I made my email devotionals and I did not even have my own book out yet. However, I was a prophetic dreamer so I knew she was not lying. I had no clue that part of my assignment as an author was not just to write my own books but to help others push out their books as well. In this divinely orchestrated instance, I was helping someone see their worth before I could see my own.

Reluctantly, I began to work on this first ever book assignment while still being afraid. I choose to trust God as I worked diligently to help this client translate their experience onto paper. I struggled so much with those first few chapters but a rhythm slowly began to develop. Every week she would give me recordings about each moment and memory of her life and my job consisted of taking notes and converting them into paragraphs. The fact that she was impressed with what was produced began to bring my confidence back to life. This was the most alive I felt in almost five years, feeling like my presence truly did matter and make a difference. Due to the size of this individual's platform, I knew I was doing a great work that was going to touch many lives, maybe even more than any of the other spaces I preached in thus far.

There were many times that her and I both faced all types of spiritual opposition such as loss, disease, betrayal, witchcraft and so much more. So many things tried to keep us both sealed in the cocoons that we were trying to push out of. However, we held those first copies of that book in our hands by October 2020. I was beyond excited for this completed project as if it was my own because it showed me just how powerful my purpose was. I was able to articulate and empathize with a lot of her story, so everything I had been through helped me express emotions for similar scenarios in her journey. The simple fact that God trusted me enough to help someone else with a book was humbling beyond comprehension. He used the gift of spreading the Gospel in a way I least expected and I suddenly became a ghostwriter.

After spending 2016 to 2020 without any form of income, He used ghostwriting to thrust me into a full-time business that I could have never saw coming. My heart was full as I began to take on more clients who needed help sharing their stories and wisdom on paper, finally giving me the fulfillment that I always longed for. It was not a skill that I learned at school because I did not get a degree in anything. It was not something any job prepared me for because I could not get a job at all. All my applications to coffee shops, supermarkets, bookstores, and more were all turned down as I suffered from shame. Finally, it was as if a dam broke and at last I had consistent income that was equivalent to that of a regular job.

I was too worried about having favor with a select few people in New Jersey but the Lord had to show me that there was so much more for me outside the small box that I felt encapsulated in. Even though I was begging God for many years to let me preach all over my region and country, He had something better in mind. Instead, He made it so that pastors, preachers, singers, politicians, entrepreneurs and other kinds of influential people are knocking my door down to book me to ghostwrite their books for them. It is a huge blessing being able to schedule my own meetings, take days off and not have to feel the anxiety and pressure of graded assignments. My only grades were God being pleased and the checks or digital payments I received every few weeks.

Before I knew it, I was soaring and allowing the wind of God to carry me with such freedom and momentum. I am just getting started but if this is how flying feels, then it was worth the brokenness. It was worth the failure, betrayal, abuse and rejection. He gave me a pen so that I could break myself free, showing me that everything I needed was on the inside of me all along. Whenever I approach my computer, I feel like a musician playing notes skillfully on their instrument, making music that will bring feelings of hope, joy, peace and enjoyment to all who will listen. I became so content with this assignment, that at one point, I told God if He was not going to let me preach anymore, I would be totally fine. The impact and testimonies of my clients' readers felt the same as if I was talking directly to them from a pulpit. However, this is just half of what my soaring season looks like.

Chapter 9

The Color of Courage

Isn't it breathtaking how nature is filled with natural color? Before we could come up with words to articulate and describe them, plants, fruits, animals, water, the sky and the stars all were filled with every color imaginable. Trees go through so many colors during the year, producing leaves that start off green and then turn red, yellow or orange. Even though all flowers start out with green stems, they can vary in the hue of their petals. Birds come in all shapes and sizes, sometimes having three or even four different colors all over their body. Then we have the butterfly who starts off as one completely different creature and then appears in a magnificent pattern of colors ranging from black, white, red, blue, orange so forth. You may have been one color in one season but it takes courage to change colors when the Lord transforms your nature.

The Lord already changed my colors when I realized I was no longer the same but it was time for me to act out my new nature and step out on faith. From 2019 to 2020, I continued to create monthly devotionals, declarations and prayers even as I worked on helping my first client with their book. Part of my routine that year was going to be attending the writing conference I went to in 2019 but that was cancelled when the coronavirus pandemic began to torment the entire world. I forgot to mention that a few months after the writing conference, I received a prophecy from a pastor all the way from the United Kingdom. He called my name and told me that everything I would do with writing was considered a job. He got more specific and said the Lord would birth a Christian writing conference out of me.

My words were few when I tried to grasp the idea that I would be making writing courses similar to the one I just attended, assuming that it would not be for another decade or so when I become established as an author. However, the pandemic a few months later forced me to take a leap of faith that I once again felt unqualified for. Who hosts a writing conference without having a book out yet? Apparently, I did and people signed up left and right. I did not know exactly how to write a full book since I was barely halfway through my client's project. However, it was my desire to share what I learned from blogging, social media posts, sermons and being able to share whatever is in your heart. I spent two whole weeks in May 2020 teaching these classes and the preacher in me resurfaced after being quiet for so long.

As I taught, prayed and encouraged people in the virtual classroom and in one-on-one phone calls, testimonies piled up as people said their minds and hearts were healed of trauma. They pushed past writer's block and finally felt the courage to let their voice be heard by documenting what God said to them. Not even a month after the conference, one of the attendees wrote a twenty-day devotional in less than two weeks. As of today, two years later, over thirty books have been written by anyone who has ever attended any of my writing classes before I wrote my own book. My willingness to walk and talk in courage helped others produce fruit.

Did I forget to mention that in addition to ghostwriting, I received major income from these writing classes?! At the end of the class, I asked for help. When I started writing those email devotionals, I had no clue that they were meant to become my first book, so I asked if the conference can help me pay my publisher. Without hesitation, they gave me twice as much what I needed to pay the publisher for my first book, which actually came into my hand one week after my client's book in October 2020 as well! So now, not only am I ghostwriter but I am a writing coach, using scriptural principles to train writers as if I was training people in ministry.

By 2021, I began to fellowship and connect with all kinds of authors from around the world. There were two who I had no clue would change the trajectory of my life in less than a year. There was a young lady who was a writing coach in one of the largest Christian writing groups on social media. She reached out to me when she saw my testimony about my second book, catching me by surprise. I wondered what she saw in me to just check up on me and pray for me periodically after that moment, until she asked me a big question. Because I wrote books in various genres, started writing classes and was a ghostwriter, she asked if I could be her personal assistant for her publishing company. My spirit leaped and accepted the invitation, now being part of someone else's publishing company in addition to having my own
company that my ghostwriting and coaching skills fell under.

Even though this was a writing company, being under opened

doors for ministry in places that I least expected, people started inviting me to preach and teach just because I was under her and they trusted her anointing and judgement. I was introduced to a whole new sphere of leaders who honored me and treated me as if I was already everything that God was making me to be. In less than a year of working with her, we recruited 100 authors for a prayer book collaboration which became the #1 Best Seller on Amazon in the Religion and Prayer categories! In addition, a major lie was broken off me, as I no longer was reduced to New Jersey. Opportunities to preach and teach on television in front of thousands of people were granted to me in March of 2022, all because I trusted God and walked with this writing coach who was one of the butterflies who replaced the moths I used to hang around.

There is yet another butterfly I began to fly with, who I met simply because I was looking for Christian authors to interview. She too had her own publishing company and was a pastor. We always talked about how the kingdom would go farther if people flew together instead of trying to outshine each other. We interviewed one another on each of our pages, prayed through all types of trials and testimonies and rejoiced at the sudden, supernatural victories that came our way. One of those victories was when the Ivy League college she graduated from invited her to speak in Fall of 2021 and secured her to do several events in 2022. They wanted her to organize a writing workshop in March of 2022 and immediately she invited me to speak at the college writing workshop alongside her.

Here I am, a college dropout who barely made it through sophomore year, failing one of the easiest degrees my school had to offer. Yet, even someone like me received a door to speak at an Ivy League college and be viewed as an expert in my craft. None of this would have happened if I was not obedient to being courageous in my craft and refusing to let what I lacked keep me from moving forward. Here I am, a preacher who was told they would never preach again a day in their life and would never grow beyond a storefront. Now, I am preaching before thousands through social media, television, and conferences on a monthly basis. I took a chance on the new colors God gave me and it caused me to find favor with those who said I was an answered prayer so that they no longer had to fly alone.

I met a caterpillar back in 2013 at a former mentor's preaching conference. I shared with you earlier that in 2018, she invited me to her prayer line where I could continue to grow in my anointing while I awaited freedom from my cocoon. Before my very eyes, she became a butterfly by walking in obedience. She too had to face similar opposition that I did but on a much greater level and that led her to creating a space that people like us needed. It was indeed a brand-new church in 2019, where she wore her new color proudly as a pastor. When the pandemic came, it gave me time to pray and reflect on my journey thus far and to see if there was any possibility for me to be in ministry again. During that season, she started asking me to preach and teach online for their virtual Sunday services and Bible studies. I was so grateful that she trusted me enough to help her, probably due to my faithfulness on the prayer line.

By the end of 2020, I was at a crossroads because of the courage I developed as I began to break free into the wind. My writing conference, ghostwriting, and my first two books gave me way more confidence than I ever had before in my life. I grew tired of hiding in the cocoon of my current church where I knew it was never going to be anything more than a gift graveyard. Right before New Year's Eve, this pastor called me and asked if I could help her by preaching once a month at her church. She did not say I had to leave my church nor did she promise me any titles or positions. However, the Lord gave me clear instructions as she talked to jump and soar. I joined her church not knowing exactly what I was doing. Immediately, there was no waiting period, as I preached on Sunday and taught Bible Study monthly from that moment onward.

It took me a while to warm up to preaching in a pulpit setting again because I was almost certain this would never happen again. As the months went by, my shell ripped open and I preached with a fire, boldness and personality that was foreign to me. I loved the new man I was becoming, the man of God I was always meant to be. By the time May 2021 rolled around, I was bombarded with a sudden announcement and I heard something I wanted to hear since I was thirteen years old. Because of the fact I was faithful on the prayer line and because she saw me grow since the day she met me, she said there was no need for me to repeat baby steps in training when I already was on a level of trustworthiness due to being trained by the wilderness.

That announcement carried me all the way until the day it was fulfilled in the summer. Sunday, August, 1st, 2021, I stood before the church in a black suit and black shirt, as my pastor inserted a white tab into my shirt's collar and officially handed me a license which officially declared that I was a minister of the Gospel of Jesus Christ. Despite every loss, heartache, delay, failure, betrayal, asthma attack, coronavirus attack and attempt to keep me sealed and silent, I soared into supernatural heights where no one could reach or hinder me. I trusted the Creator's tailor-made process for my life, trusted and believed that He would take my tears and use them as rain to water the garden that I could fly around in. As you have read this short summary of my journey, please know that if God gave me the courage to fly, He will do the same for you. Let Him do His work and watch His glory change your story from broken to blessed.

Even in moments of fear, frustration and even failure, God would always remind me to use my faith to focus on His favor! Even butterflies can have PTSD and claustrophobia after they have broken free of their shell but life does not always naturally line up with where you currently are spiritually. The moth of hell named Satan will always try to make you walk in imposter syndrome making you believe you are a moth or that you are still a caterpillar who is not truly free, marvelous, successful or in right standing in God. When you are in the desert place, that can be the tunnel between trauma and triumph as you leave your prison land for the promised land. However, you must be mindful that God does not do half miracles and would not heal, transform and glorify you just for you to fly around aimlessly.

You are flying with a purpose and there are flowers of favor, trees of testimony, plants of promise and skyscrapers of supernatural success and sustainment that you can only reach now that you have your wings. If you still find yourself in the caterpillar or cocoon stage, you need to think yourself into transformation. The Bible says in Proverbs 3:27 that *as a man thinks in his heart, so is he*. Vice versa, if you are a butterfly but still bound to caterpillar and cocoon mindsets, behaviors and insecurities, you will stay stuck and stagnant, weakening your worth and possibly your will to live! I have endured this war for a long time, as it would be easy for me to feel like I am still a failure, still broken and still not in God's will. Because of the nature of my work as a ghostwriter, I have so many private victories that cannot wash away the public failures that many have watched me endure.

It hurts when people assume you are still the old version of yourself when your progress is not tangible to them based on your education, financial status and even relationship status. However, what has been so comforting for me is that God made a covenant with me that I was not even aware of. All of 2022, while writing this book, it seemed like I would hear more sermons about butterflies than ever before. Butterflies of all colors, mostly orange, would find me and land on me wherever I go, reminding me that my metamorphosis is just getting started. Like it says in 1 John 3:2, *it has not yet appeared what I shall be.* Between now and the day Jesus comes back for His church, I will be transforming and evolving many times during the rest of this life as I await the promise of a perfect body so that I can live in a perfect world with no pain, fear, sorrow, depression or loneliness. Christ has a covenant and contract with you that calls you to embrace the divine blueprint that God has set aside for you. Trust Him with every single moment of your life and I promise you, you will soar like never before!

Kimberly Stratton
Author, Prayer Warrior,
Pastor, CEO and Founder of
International H.O.P.E. Inc.
and The Crown And Cross
Consulting And Publishing
Company, LLC

The Egg Stage

Chapter 1

In The Beginning

Our natural life is very similar to the evolution of the butterfly. We think we're not worthy and we get fed what we feel is garbage or are nurtured with substances beneath us. At times it seems lonely but God has a beautiful plan written especially for us. We may have to crawl on our bellies sometimes slow and steady but soon we will learn how to fly with grace and beauty toward our purpose and path God has destined for us.

Lets talk about the beginning. How does a butterfly come to be? The first stage of a butterfly's life cycle is called the egg stage. This process is where the female butterfly will search for an adequate home to lay her eggs. The home usually consists of a leaf or some type of stem so that the eggs are somewhat safe, able to survive and grow so they can eventually hatch. The egg, (prior to hatching), starts the form of a caterpillar and once released, devours the nutrients in its surroundings (the leaf or stem) in order to grow and develop into the next stage. We know that inside of that egg is the caterpillar that is waiting to spring forth but just like the beginning stages of a baby, the caterpillar is not recognizable. It doesn't look like a caterpillar. Again, the same way a baby in the early stages of the first trimester (roughly the first 12 weeks of a woman's pregnancy) is unrecognizable. It doesn't look like a baby. However, as time goes on, the process takes place. With more development, foreign matter eventually reveals something recognizable – a caterpillar or a baby. Now I will not go into full details regarding the butterfly's egg stage and how long it takes for the egg to develop into the caterpillar which develops into the pupa and then into the adult stage. Nor will I go into full details regarding the stages of a woman's pregnancy and how a baby develops. I will leave that to your parents, sex education: pregnancy and lepidoptery – the study of butterflies; however, I will touch upon the similarities of the butterfly and our life cycle as it relates to our walk and development with God.

Growing up was pretty average for me or at least I thought. Like the female butterfly in search of a nurturing and adequate home to lay her eggs, my mom searched for the same – an adequate home to have her baby girl. As a pregnant teenager, she didn't have the full support of her family, friends nor my dad to encourage her to keep and protect the life that formed and grew inside of her. In the beginning stages of her pregnancy, my mom had a very athletic body and didn't show the life growing inside of her, initially. She knew she carried a baby girl because the Lord spoke to her and told her. Grateful for a baby girl even at such a young age, my mom understood how special I was. Not everyone saw the specialness of a pregnant teen in the beginning but isn't that just like life? Of the hundreds of thousands of butterflies in the world, all different shapes, sizes and colors people still have their favorite(s). They select their favorite butterfly based on *their* favorite color, the size or the shape or the butterfly or even the species but not realizing that every single butterfly is special. Regardless of the species, the color, the shape or other distinguishing features, each and every single butterfly is special and uniquely created. No two butterflies – just like people – are exactly the same. That is how God created us. Unique. Different. Special in our own way. Twins – even if they are identical – are not the exact same. One may have a slightly smaller or slightly larger face or has a distinct feature or quality that the other doesn't have. That uniqueness breathed into each of us as God's children makes us individualistic and just like the butterfly, He created us all special; even if no one else can see it, God can.

Unfortunately, like most adults and family members as well as others, my grandmom couldn't see my uniqueness in my mom's preteen womb. When she found out my mom was pregnant, my grandmom (after she confirmed that my mom was pregnant) made an appointment with the doctor's office but not just any doctor. She made an appointment with a doctor at an abortion clinic unbeknownst to my mom. My grandmom went so far as to actually take my mom to an abortion clinic and attempted to strap my mom down to start the procedure but the doctor and nurses were no match for the strength the Lord gave my mom. She fought, kicked and attempted to cause physical harm to the next person who tried to take her unborn baby girl. The doctor and nurses gave up and told my grandmom to take my mom out of there before she scared the other women. My mom was victorious. As my mom's body morphed and changed, eating habits altered and vomiting ensued, it was hard to not notice a pregnant teen around the house, at the bus stop and at school. No matter what, my mom promised to love and care for me at all costs even when everyone around her advised her to abort me. See, the female butterfly has made a similar promise to her eggs as well. Obviously, without saying so, she has promised to love and care for her eggs at all costs, protect them from danger and find suitable housing and food for them once they hatch. The female butterfly can't just find any home, place or leaf to lay her eggs. She must try and make sure the surrounding area is safe and full of nutrients that the caterpillar can feed on once it hatches. The area must be free from threats not only looking to kill the female butterfly but to devour her eggs as well. The female butterfly must kick, fight and attempt to take out anything and anyone who tries to eat, destroy or cause her to abort her eggs.

I love this analogy of my protective mother and the protective female butterfly. Both are carrying precious cargo that neither want to be ruined, damaged or destroyed. It makes me think about a person coming to Christ and dedicating their life to Him for the first time. We call them "babes (abbreviated for baby) in Christ". We call them babes because they have not yet learned how to walk. They are in the egg or beginning stage. They have given their life to Christ and are experiencing a new life, a new walk, a new talk, a new set of eyes and a reset of their life. They are still trying to understand how their sins are washed away, how the sea of forgetfulness works and how to truly walk in the newness of life. They are learning how to crawl around in their new territory and are curious about their walk, path and destiny in Christ. They are looking towards the more seasoned and wise Saints on how to speak, dress, praise, worship, read God's word and acquire a new attitude by turning the other cheek. Just like a baby needs the nutrients of milk to help them grow and develop, babes in Christ need the sincere milk of God's Word in order to help them grow and develop. At times babes need to be cuddled, reassured and taught lessons multiple times until it sinks in for them. They need to be protected at all costs so the initial fire they have will not be extinguished or caused to go out too quickly. Babes must learn to pace themselves as well.

Whether it's an egg, a caterpillar, a baby or a babe in Christ, they share similarities and there's a beginning and ending stage for each. The common denominator they all share is God. God created each with a life cycle. Just like a butterfly, they are all unique, beautifully created and will evolve into their full purpose.

The Larva Stage

Chapter 2

Feed Me. I Am Hungry

Just like every butterfly's birth and every woman's pregnancy is different, so is everyone's growth and spiritual journey with God. What works for you, may not work for another. What worked for me, may not work for you. Does that mean that my growth and spiritual journey with God is less or more superior to yours? Does that mean that a butterfly who is left in the cocoon a little bit longer to complete its process is any more or less superior to another butterfly? Does that mean that one woman's pregnancy and having her baby at 36 weeks or 40 or 42 weeks is more or less superior to another? No. In each of those scenarios, God's timing is perfect. The second stage of a butterfly's life cycle is the larva or caterpillar stage. You can equate this stage to months 3 through 6 of a woman's pregnancy – if you're keeping track that is. I like to call this the time as the Bible so eloquently puts it, " *he that hungers and thirsts after righteousness shall be filled*." So fitting as the title *Feed Me. I Am hungry*.

After being cramped up in that small, tiny egg and then finally hatching to be released, the caterpillar or larvae is famished.

This is the stage where the caterpillar just eats, and eats, and eats and eats. It's a constant process of eating, shedding, growing, eating, shedding, growing and repetition of those three processes. Not only does the caterpillar eat its way out of the egg but it continues to eat the surrounding area the female butterfly found adequate to lay her eggs. Again, the home usually consists of a leaf or some type of stem so that the eggs are somewhat safe, able to survive and grow so they can eventually hatch. The egg, (prior to hatching), starts the form of a caterpillar and once released, devours the nutrients in its surroundings (the leaf or stem) in order to grow and develop in the current stage as well as the next stage. It's pretty much the stage prior to hibernation that bears go through. As we've learned on the discovery channels, bears will gorge on food and store up fat so they can sleep comfortably through the winter without having to go out and forage for food. Same with the butterfly and the same with the baby that's now forming in the mother's womb. Again, months 3 through 6 of a woman's pregnancy is a crucial time and sometimes known as the golden time. Many women feel their body starting to shape, better form, less back pain, better sleep, increased energy and drive including increased appetite and less nausea. Many pregnant women have said they felt hungry all the time during this golden time and can eat any and everything they want; while mixing and combining various food that the average person would never consider combining (such as ice cream and pickles, clam chowder and Doritos, Nutella and Twizzlers, chalk, sand, dark chocolate covered bacon, spicy food and the list goes on). This is the same again with the caterpillar who eats, sheds and grows.

I know some of you are wondering how and what does this have to do with babes in Christ? Well, think about it. In the womb, the baby is consuming every sustenance the mother is taking in. That's one of the reasons why the mother is so hungry all the time and not just hungry but devouring any and every kind of food in her path. Well, babes in Christ are the same way. When a babe comes off the street and starts attending church services and is around the Saints, the babe starts taking in their new scenery. The babe starts simulating and noticing how the members of the church dress, walk, talk, their lifestyle and babes notice if Saints are or are not different from the world they just came out of. Babes in Christ hunger and thirst after righteousness and are looking to devour as many Christlike examples as they can so they can absorb and be filled more with Christlike ways. They emulate the examples that are presented before them. Remember Saints we are walking epistles as the Word of God tells us. Babes will consume the Word of God and ask questions. They will not be so easily shunned or easily cast to the side or accept any tomfoolery. They are seeking realness. Among many things, they hunger for the Bread of Life and the Word of God; a newness in themselves. This can only be given by Christ, the love and nourishment from the Body of Christ and the sound doctrine of God not man. I recall when the Lord called me. At first, I was skeptical. I wasn't sure if it was God calling me because of all the self-righteous and fake Saints (or shall I say Aints) that I knew, the examples I saw from Aints who talked a good talk about living a righteous life but sipped on the bottle right after church services, played lottery, stood in line for their numbers, gossiped about who saw what, who wore what, slept with who and things of that nature. I was skeptical because I saw a form of godliness and everyone had righteousness in their own eyes. I saw the husbands cheat on the wives and the wives looked at the young boys while their husbands looked at the young girls. I saw the broken homes including the very one my family grew up in. They Aints talked a good talk but when it came down to it, it was a bunch of lip service and hypocrisy. I wanted to be real for God. I didn't want to have one foot or one toe in the world and the other parts of my body pretend to serve God, slobbered on the altar Sunday but then Monday night ready to get jiggy with it. So, when I finally accepted the call of Christ in my life and realized it was Christ, I ran into the church doors and gave my all to God. I was hungry for him. I didn't realize how thirsty I was until He provided me with a cup of water that I shall never thirst again and as I drank that cup of water, the living waters that flowed throughout my body replenished my soul. It made me never want to turn my back on God again. See my story is not like most and God told me that if went back into the world (because He waited like a gentleman for 12 long years for me), I would surely die. Some may say that wasn't the literal meaning but I want you to know that I was not in a position to mock, negotiate nor play semantics with God. I knew the Lord meant that if I went back into the world after He patiently and lovingly waited for me for 12 long years and saved me from my sin and shame and if I went back out and chose the devil over Him, He would surely end my life. I had (and still have) such a hunger, thirst and run like fire shut up in my bones for the Lord, that I couldn't go back. I wouldn't go back. I won't go back. It’s different when you know, that you know, that you know. I was different when God called me and that difference made me stand out. That difference made me walk a little bit more Christlike. That difference made me talk a little bit more Christlike. Many saw the gifts in me including leadership but refused to tell me what they saw. Instead, they wanted to pimp out the gifts that God gave me for their own benefit and how dare I resign from their ministry when the Lord gave me my marching orders to leave. He let me know that I outgrew the fishbowl that I was in and it was time to move on because the ground was tainted or lessons learned. I received what I was supposed to receive and then shook the dust off my feet. I will never forget a prophecy I received when I returned to God in 2010. I was told that I was peculiar but not just simply the peculiar people as the Bible speaks of but the Lord specifically said that I have a peculiar journey and walk with Him that many will not understand and will actually call me “weird” at times because I was set apart, consecrated and a peculiar people. My journey would not be easy but the Lord would always be with me. I've held on to that since 2010 because the prophecy has shown to be true. Many don't understand my walk even though

God sends me under leaders that I've excelled above in the spiritual realm and they don't understand why. To be clear, I'm not bragging on myself. I'm bragging on the gifts that the Lord has provided me. I'm just bragging on my God. During this time frame in my life, I have been so hungry for the Lord that natural food lost its flavoring. I've been so thirsty for the Lord in a dry and weary land that no amount of liquids on this earth can quench my desire for Him. I want to be so wrapped up, so tied up and so tangled up in the Lord that when He says, "he that hungers and thirsts after righteousness shall be filled" that only He can fill my spirit. I understand the hunger that the caterpillar has to escape from the egg to get into a world to start its journey. I understand the unborn baby that's inside the mother's womb who's devouring every nutrient that it possibly can so that it can sustain itself once it is released into the world. I am the butterfly. I am the creation of my master. I am beautiful, unique, fearfully and wonderfully made. I am honored to have been called "peculiar" – it is my birthright. I don't take this walk and journey that I've experienced with the Lord for granted. Everyone's growth and spiritual journey with God is different. I walk in my butterfly evolution because the Lord has taken me from broken to blessed.

Chapter 3

My Testimony

All of God's people have a testimony whether they want to believe it or not or whether they want to tell their testimony or not. The book of Revelations tells us that *they overcame him by the blood of the lamb and by the word of their testimony and they loved not their lives unto death.* I love that scripture! It lets us know that we gained victory (we're conquerors) by the blood of the lamb and the word of our testimony because we did not love our life or try to hold onto it but instead had faith when faced with death. We may not face a natural death every day because obviously we can only die once in this natural body; however, in the spiritual realm, the enemy tries its best to decapitate us. He tries over and over and over again to end our life in the spiritual so it that it's a reflection in the natural. Many shrink away at the thought of this and are so frightened and paralyzed that they do not even utter their testimony. That is a direct violation of the Word of God. I was always taught by the older Saints then if you can't stand up and give a testimony on the goodness of the Lord, just simply raise and wave your hand and we all understood what that motion meant. But I also remember a song they sang that said, "I said I wasn't gonna testify but I couldn't keep it to myself what the Lord has done for me." I have so many testimonies of what the Lord has done for me, how good He has been to me, how He spared my life so many times when I thought it was mine to do what I wanted; yet, He was so patient, loving, merciful and forgiving. I have so many testimonies that it seems like every time someone is going through a trial, tribulation, situation or whatever the case may be, that I have a testimony on how I got over and how my soul looks back and wonder how I got over. But it was just by His amazing grace and reckless love for me.

I think the best testimony to start off is to tell you how the Lord spared my life even in my mom's womb. Never mind the fact that everybody in my family wanted my mother to abort me because it was not popular in the 70s to be a pregnant, unwed teen. The devil also tried to take me out when man's plan to abort me did not work. Once, my grandmom, Theresa realized that my mom was not going to abort me and was ready to mud-stomp a hole in anyone who tried to make her abort me, my grandmom gave up and authorized medical care for my mom and I. As the time came closer to my mom's due date (apparently, I was born earlier than expected but again, God's timing is perfect), the devil tried to take me out and had the umbilical cord wrapped around my neck. Of course, this placed my mom in distress as well as myself and the doctors were so anxious to try to get me born into the world that they almost participated and choked the life out of me. Finally realized that I was breeched, they turned me around and I was born into the world but without a sound. After a few moments they worked on me and tried to get me to come to life. A final smack on the bottom released the grip on my neck, the air from my lungs and I wailed. I wasn't unscathed. The markings of the cord lightly darkened the area around my neck even to this day. Clearly, the devil had plans to take me out knowing that I would be a force to be reckoned with once I knew whom I belong to, the purpose and calling all my life and not only believed and had faith but moved in that calling. The devil was so scared at the thought of me realizing that I am a child of God that he tried to take me out; kill me before I was even born. Others have this testimony as well. The devil wanted you to die before you came into the knowledge and truth of whom you belong to. Unfortunately, some are still sleeping while others straddle the fence. Then there are those who know the calling on their life but they're just not ready. I was there at one point in time. Just know that once you come to the realization, no matter how much time you try to make up, you will never make up that lost time. So don't try. What also brought me to the realization was the number of souls that were waiting on me. Waiting on me to say yes to God, waiting on me to get my life right with God so that they could hear one of my many testimonies and be encouraged to know that if God did it for me, then surely He will do it for them. Someone right now is waiting on your testimony to hear how you got over and that you don't look like what you've been through. I've heard people (including myself) say, *"well I need to get myself together first."* That doesn't make sense. If you could get yourself together, then why would you need God or Jesus at all? You'd have all the answers.

Again, I have testimonials for days. We can fast forward many years later to a time when I trusted the catty, mean and envious girls in high school – not realizing that I was being set up for the setup. There was this one particular catty, mean girl (more envious of me than mean) who pretended to befriend me and tried to set me up with someone else's boyfriend. At the time she clearly knew I didn't know these two individuals were dating. But again catty high schoolers right? Nonetheless, she invited me out one evening to hang out and I was like cool. She did the whole introduction between the guy and I and he was a guy (high school boys will be high school boys sad to say). Nonetheless, fast forward to later that evening and the guy and I hook up. Unbeknownst to me the girlfriend (who didn't like me but in high school do they really need a reason to dislike you?) was called and told that I was with her man. Thankfully the grace of God got me out of that particular situation but the following day the girlfriend came to school to shoot me over her boyfriend. Thankfully, a teacher stopped her in her tracks as she searched for me because she was in the wrong place during school hours. The teacher let me know what was going down and I was just shocked. Of course, the catty, mean girl played completely innocent in all of this but I knew to keep my distance. The sad part is this is not even an unusual story because of the world and society we live in today. People have been known to tailgate and get upset when a person break-checks them only to pull up to the next traffic light or stop sign, pull out a gun and either shoot or threaten to shoot the brake checker.

One of the last testimonies for this section (because again I could go on for days) is where I almost took my own life with no help from the devil. Obviously thinking I was grown and one of the big girls, I hung out with the big dogs – grown men who clearly had no business out with high schoolers. They brought us drinks and we partied, hung out, drank all night and partied until the wee hours in the morning. I promise you we probably drank as they smoked weed from after school until like 6 in the morning. I drove back home in my mom's car, bobbed and weaved across lanes of traffic due to being exhausted, sleep deprived and almost alcohol poisoned as much as we drank and didn't eat. As I closed my eyes for a few seconds on my way driving back home, a tractor-trailer came towards me. It was nobody but the hand of God that took the steering wheel and steered me back into my lane as the tractor-trailer blared its horn. I heard none of this. I was in such a deep sleep that by the time I realized all that happened, the steering wheel had placed me back in my lane and the tractor-trailer laid on its horn and passed by me. I literally don't remember my hands on the steering wheel. You would have thought that woke me up and scared me straight. No, it didn't. Thankfully I was just a mile from home but I hear that most accidents happen one mile from your home. Like I said, unfortunately, that did not scare me straight but that was the last night that I stayed out all hours of the night and drank and partied. I still drank and partied but didn't stay out all night long as before. I share these few testimonies to say that during my life, God had already chosen my path. Before the drinking and driving and before the sexual relationships and bad decisions and choices I made, God knew my yes would be yes and **when** my yes would be my yes. When I think of all that the Father endured and the angels that He sent my way to help me through treacherous decisions that I made and didn't hold any of that over my head but still showed me grace and mercy; still allowed me to live another day unharmed. Many don't have that testimony. I am grateful. I thank God that he did not see me where I was but saw me where I would be standing before Him declaring that He is my Father and I His child. I stand before you this day a woman of God, saved, baptized, filled with the precious gift of the Holy Ghost and can speak in tongues as the Lord gives utterance; sanctified, I got Jesus on my mind and running for my life.

Chapter 4

What God Has For You Is For You

I used to hear this saying, "what God has for you, is for you." I would also hear people (Saints and others) say do not tell people your business because they will stop God's plan(s) for you. Let's make up our minds. Which one is it? Are we saying that *what God has for an individual is for that individual* or are we saying that *that individual is so powerful and so above God and can tell God what to do that if they commanded, whatever God has for you can be stopped*? Now, trust me. I absolutely understand not telling people your business because they can go to man and get man to not move on your behalf or no longer find favor with you. I've had that happen to me (testimony). However, it can only be one way or the other. Either we trust God and His promises or we believe that man is more powerful than God. We can't have it both ways and then try to slick talk and use scripture to get around either saying. I'm going to stand and make a declaration that what God has for you is for you and what God has for me is for me and neither one of us can convince God to do ANYTHING! We as Christians can't say that the Lord formed the earth and breathe breath into the nostrils of man that he created from dirt and at the same time place man on such a high pedestal that man can actually deter the hand and move of God? Silliness. I do believe that there is a season and a time for everything as the Bible tells us. There's a time to laugh and a time to cry; a time to mourn and a time to reap; a time to sow and a time to go through trials and tribulations and at the same time to bask in the fruit thereof. But I refuse to believe that any person can move the hand of God. Period!

I can speak all of this with certainty because I believe in the Word of God. There's no scripture in the 66 books of the King James Bible that says that man can turn the hand of God. If that's the case, the story would be written a little bit differently. I can speak all of this with certainty because as I grew up, death was spoken over my life by my very own family. The very ones meant to protect me, to nurture me, to love me and to care for me. Not only was death spoken over me but I was called names that I was not such as lazy, dumb, ignorant, stupid and the list goes on. If I chose to believe that what man has for me is for me, I would believe at the age of seven or eight that I was a Jezebel. At that age, I didn't even know how to spell the word, didn't know what it meant but the way it was spoken over my life and spoken to me, made me know that it was not a good thing. I can count on the number of fingers, on one hand, the number of gracious, merciful, loving and kind words my family spoke over my life. I can't however count on any of my hands, fingers, toes of mine and my neighbors and neighbors and neighbors of the loving, kind, gentle and encouraging words my mom and grandmom spoke over my life. Please understand there's a distinction between family and the trio (my mom, my grandmom and I).

Do I believe that God means to do us any harm? Absolutely not. He tells us in His word in Jeremiah 29:11 of the prosperous, good things and good future that He has in store for us. There is not one place in God's Word does He speak to do us ill or harm. He is our master; our craftsman. Yes, the Bible speaks in earlier times when God says He was disappointed in man and regretted the day that He ever created man but then God stumbled upon Noah and his family and man had a reset; a new beginning. The Bible tells us that gifts and callings come without repentance. Look at God's graciousness! God already prepared and planned a purpose for our life and equipped us not only with the Fruit of the Spirit, not only with His Holy Spirit to lead us and to guide us as well as the other many other duties the Holy Spirit has but He also provided us and instilled in us gifts to equip and edify the Body of Christ. Those gifts also are meant to help and serve us in our walk and journey with Christ as well. God has more than equipped us and again Him being there for us because He says in His Word that He will never leave us nor forsake us. We are the ones that leave and forsake God. We are the ones who treat Him like Elf on a Shelf and pick Him up and put Him down and position Him how we want; when we want. The amazing thing about God is that even when we falter, fall get off track and try to lead ourselves down our own path, He is right there to lead us and guide us as a Good Shepherd back on the straight and narrow – the road less traveled. He is right there to send angels to tell us to go in the direction that we should go or that we are on the right track. Amazingly enough, even when we falter or go the wrong way God, God does not hold grudges. We may have to do a little extra work, ask for repentance and get on the right track with Him but thank God that God does not keep tabs. He will still continue to help us find our purpose in life as long as we submit ourselves to Him.

So, the next time someone wants to add their two cents and

try to sell you on their rendition of what God does and does not have for you, just tell them, **it is written** the Lord already has my past, present, future, purpose and destiny pre-written. Then quote Jeremiah 29:11 and bid them a good day! No longer allow anyone to have power nor control over your life and destiny because again it is already pre-written what God has for you, is for you.

The Pupa/Chrysalis "transition" Stage

Chapter 5

My Cocoon

In high school science class and in certain college courses, we learned about butterflies, their life cycle and the evolution of the caterpillar to the actual butterfly. My favorite stage in the butterfly's process was the cocoon. The cocoon or chrysalis stage is where the caterpillar forms a protective layer around itself. This protective layer is called a pupa. During the pupa stage, the pupa goes through multi-layer conversions or changes. Throughout this development, the chrysalis protects the pupa and in roughly 2 weeks, the pupa completes its metamorphosis and transforms into an exquisite butterfly. I love the cocoon stage because, to me, the cocoon protects, encases and keeps the caterpillar safe. It isolates the caterpillar from the rest of the world, all its dangers, he said, she said, insecurities, envy, doubt, self-doubt, hatred, predators and so forth. The only way the cocoon does not protect the caterpillar is if something penetrates the cocoon; interrupts its development, process and peace. This self-time the caterpillar has can be foreseen as isolation.

Countless people misconstrue the serenity of isolation and

think it's a bad thing; however, isolation is not always bad. Isolation can be shielding yourself from others, setting yourself apart from the drama and placing healthy boundaries between you and others to keep your sanity. Isolation can also be used to keep yourself away from sick people and their contagious self-absorbed, woahest me, I am a victim-type mentality. There are several times mentioned in the Bible that Jesus had to isolate himself from not only the crowd, those He healed, the Sadducees and Pharisees but also the disciples. There were times that He had to get away so that He and his Father could commune and Jesus could be rejuvenated and restored for the journey ahead.

Just like the butterfly, my cocoon forms a protective layer around me. My cocoon are those individuals that I trust with my life, my finances, the keys to my house and everything that I hold dear. My cocoon aka my circle is very small and tight-knit. I always say that my circle is so small that it's a period. My cocoon are those individuals that pray for me, have my best interest at heart, speak truth to me no matter what, are godly counsel and always have my back. They support me in more ways than I know. That support comes in countless ways such as praying for me when I don't know they're praying, when I asked for prayer or just having a sense that I need them. That support can be financial, mental, emotional and so forth. That support is also reciprocal. The amazing part about my cocoon is that they're all from different walks of my life whether it stemmed from a friendship over 30 plus years ago that turned into my bestie and bloomed into a sisterhood. To my Stroudsburg Sister in Christ and the new Sister in Christ that both war fared and prayed with me in seasons of spiritual uproar. To my 2nd Brother in Christ whom I met in a season of my life and even though I'm much older than he, we went through very similar tragedies and now look at us collaborating on this book. To the Mother of Zion whom I've had the liberty the publishing her book and when God had her pray for me she anointed my feet (literally) before I started my journey to Florida. To my Sister in Christ (with living waters that flow through her) who helped me reach God's people and assisted me with my very first church auxiliary. To my SIC/SWISS/SweetSis (she knows whom she is based on those letters alone) and to my 1st Lil Bro in Christ (he knows who he is). My cocoon consists of those who know they can rely on me and I can rely on them because time has shown us and most importantly, my Mom. All of whom are my cocoon; my protectors; my armor bearers.

Please understand that not everyone can be in your cocoon or your inner circle; your inner tribe. The cocoon is a specially reserved place. Not everyone can have or gain access nor is it meant for everyone to gain or have access. What I have learned in life is that we will call people our friends when really they are not. They barely deserve the category of associate. Just because you socialize with them when you need, doesn't entitle them to a role or title in your life. We are so quick to put people in the "friend" category and say, "that's my friend" and that individual hasn't even placed you in that category. As a matter of fact, they're calling you an associate – if that. We must be ever so careful of the titles and roles that we give to individuals so carelessly and so freely. The trust that we extend to others, are they extending it back? The position and role that we so freely give others, do they reserve that position, role or title for you? You may say the answer is yes but have you asked them? Let's be clear, Jesus had the 12 disciples but he had the inner core as well. Read the Word of God. How many disciples were allowed at the transfiguration? Yes, Jesus allowed all the disciples to come with Him to the Garden of Gethsemane but how many went into the inner circle of the garden while Jesus asked them to watch while He prayed? When it came time to raise the deceased daughter of the Roman soldier, who did Jesus call into the inner room? Just because you meet someone and may or may not be their friend, does not mean you're friends for life. Just because at one point in time someone is in your circle, doesn't mean they're always meant to be in your circle. I truly believe that some people have a season in your life. That season can be for a day, a week, a month, a year or more but allow what is meant to take place, to take place. We need to stop holding on to people and things that are only meant for a brief season (maybe a week or a month) not years. You will know the difference. While you're playing checkers, they're playing chess. Again, I'm grateful for my cocoon. Enough said.

Chapter 6

I Am A Vessel of God

I am a firm believer that in order to know where you're going, you must know where you came from and you must understand the path that is set before you. It may not be easy to find out where you came from and once you do, it may be a hard pill to swallow. There may be some held-back truths that are unveiled that you thought you weren't ready to face – but did. You may not understand the path that is set before you but just know that your "yes" means yes. Your yes represents your yes to God. That is all you will ever need to forge ahead and create your own footprints in the sand; create your own trail off the beaten path; the narrow roadway; the road less traveled and followed. You must understand that your yes to God will dictate your path. You must also understand that God will use your footprints to help others hike that same trail you walked and survived. I remember reading a very powerful post on social media. The father said to the son, "be careful where you walk." The son responded to the father, "you be careful where you walk. Remember that I follow in your footsteps." There are souls waiting ***on us*** and ***for us*** to say yes to God in order for them to be a vessel to be used by Him. God wants to use you to help create a new set of "real" footprints for others to follow. God will use our feet to build a new path for others to walk in or be a bridge to help others cross troubled water. Some may say why me? Others may say no, not me but I beg to differ. Instead of saying why me, say why not me. There is something in each and every one of us that God can use. The Word of God lets us know that *all things work together for the good of them that love the Lord and are called according to His purpose.* I love God. I trust His plan and purpose for my life. I humbly say yes and ask God to continue to use me as a vessel, a conduit to do His will and His way. My name is Kimberly Stratton and I am a servant and follower of Jesus Christ as well as a vessel to be used by God who has allowed me to flourish in countless ways. I am not ashamed of Him or the gospel. For some who may know me and for some who may not, let me introduce myself.

I am saved, sanctified, fire baptized and filled with the precious gift of the Holy Ghost. I will speak in tongues as the Lord gives utterance.

I am a multi-self-published author

I am the CEO and Founder of a faith-based feeding program called International H.O.P.E. Inc.. The H.O.P.E. stands for Helping Overcome Poverty Everywhere.

I am the CEO and Founder of my very own consulting and publishing company called The Crown And Cross Consulting And Publishing Company LLC.

In my journey with God, He has ordained me as a Pastor; I am a spiritual mentor, a godmother to several beautiful and wonderful children (and some adults) and more. I am excited for not just my past journey and how far God has brought me but for the future that God saw in me and all those souls He allowed and still allows me to assist in any way possible.

I am a:

Servant to the Most High God

a Speakerbox for God

Foretold Apostolic Ministry

Prophetess in training and speaking only thus saith the Lord

Warrior for Christ

Soul winner for the Kingdom ~ locally and abroad

Intercessor

Prayer Warrior

Appointed and anointed

Blessed and highly favored

The apple of God's eye

Woman of Virtue

God's Scroll

Gift of Healing and Discernment

5 Fold Ministry called

at least a 5th Generational Dreamer and interpreter of dreams

Elder

Evangelist

Missionary

Deaconess

Usher

Finance Keeper of the Church

Prior Pastor's Assistant

Confidant

Friend

Sister

Daughter

Godmother

Good godly counsel

Storyteller

Woman and encourager of God and so much more.

God has used me in a variety of ways and over the years I have learned very valuable lessons concerning vessels. For one, in order to be a vessel, you must be willing. God is a gentleman and He will never force Himself on you. He will never force you to do something you don't want to do. Yes, God may take you out of your comfort zone but He wants you to have free will. He makes it very clear in His word to choose you this day whom you will serve. Then He goes on to say that He hopes that you choose life so that He can give it to you abundantly. The other thing that I have learned (and it's a very important lesson) is that as a willing vessel, you can't dictate when you will and won't be willing. You can't create your own contract with God. You can't give Him anything less than 100% of yourself. Anything less than 100% of you isn't all of you and God wants all of you. You may ask how can you become a vessel to be used by God? The first thing is to establish a relationship with Him. Take time out of your day, multiple times a day, to converse with God. Talk with God but also listen. We tend to feel awkward in the uncomfortable silence. That's the time to tune in to God, lower the volume on the noise and all the distractions around you. Another way to become a vessel to be used by God is to read His Word, study His Word, meditate on His Word and keep His commandments. Be holy for He is holy. Taste your words before they are spoken. Be not only a hearer but a doer of God's Word. Don't just give God lip service and put on a show for the people of God and the world. Walk the walk and talk the talk. Be righteous. Uplift and build versus tearing down and destroying. Most of all, if you do not have the Holy Spirit, tarry for it as the Word of God tells us. Another key point with a vessel is that you need to be able to hold the oil that God has given you. Yes times may get rough and tough and you may feel like giving up and throwing in the towel but you must hold on to the hem of His garment. You must literally say to God, "Lord hold on to me when I feel I can't hold on to you - when I feel as if I'm hanging on by a string." You must gird up your loins and put on the whole armor of God so that you can withstand the fiery darts and the wiles of the devil. Above all, when you feel that you need to be encouraged, other than picking up your Word, praying and seeking the Lord's face, assemble yourself with the Saints of God to be strengthened during those times. The devil wants the sheep to think they're weak and start to drift off alone but not so said God. Vessels need to make sure they're constantly oiling up their whole armor, spiritually fueling their Holy Spirit and making sure that they are not chipped and full of cracks where the enemy can slide in and produce turmoil in you from the inside out. Your armor will get bruised. You will have fiery darts aimed and shot at you. Some darts may hit and some may miss but prayer will keep your armor intact. Last but not least, know that the race is not given to the swift nor the strong but he that endures until the end. Endure until the end.

Chapter 7

Growth and Development

Throughout my sections of the book, I have made 3 parallels: the life cycle of a butterfly in comparison to a woman's pregnancy as compared to babes in Christ. I have correlated the differences between all three individually and how they are similar to one another. The same way each stage in the life cycle of a butterfly is pertinent to its growth and development is the same way each stage or trimester is pertinent to an unborn baby's growth and development prior to entering the world and the same with the love and care given to babes in Christ for their growth and development in not only their walk with one another but their walk with God.

All stages in the life cycle of a butterfly (from the egg to the caterpillar, to the pupa/chrysalis to the adult and so forth) are geared towards its growth and development; however the first three stages, for me, weigh more heavily than the last stages. Think about it. In order for the butterfly to have proper growth and development, there needs to be adequate preparation and nourishment. The female butterfly again searches for a home, a location so that her eggs will have a place to safely survive, hatch and receive all of the nutrients needed to feed causing the shedding of the caterpillar to morph and grow enough for the pupa stage. Without a safe and secure home and environment, the eggs will not survive and will die. Hence the end of the cycle. If the caterpillar does not feed and gorge on enough food, it will not get "fat" enough to create the outer layer for the chrysalis stage. As the caterpillar is completely inside the pupa or the cocoon stage, it's no longer feeding externally. Everything that the caterpillar ate prior, is what it will rely on for its nourishment, growth and development. There is no opportunity for the caterpillar to come out of the pupa stage to feed again to gain enough strength to create the pupa for the next stage. The same way with an unborn baby in the mother's womb. I talked about the second trimester where the mother will just feed and eat her heart's desire not only because she has her appetite back and not only because she's feeding for at least her and the baby but she must feed so that the baby receives all the nutrients required to grow and develop. As the mother feeds, the baby takes every single nutrient from her where she may lack but the unborn baby will not. Just like the butterfly, the unborn baby does not have the opportunity to step outside of its wound to eat its own selection of food so it can gain nourishment, grow and develop. Both the caterpillar and the unborn baby in the womb, are dependent upon the prior process to ensure its growth and development. Just like babes in Christ, as I discussed previously when they come into the church, they are hungry and thirsty for righteousness. They have questions. They are seeking answers to those questions. They are not just simply accepting "do as I say and not as I do" but they are looking for examples of realness. They are looking for examples of those truly following Christ for their growth and development. As they emulate the Saints, they are looking to build their own version of themselves to be Christlike and to be like a moth to a flame – draw people in.

When creating an analogy between the three of these topics (butterflies, unborn babies, and babes in Christ), you may distinguish between the word "growth" and the word "development." Growth can be seen as the exterior increase. Obviously, in female butterflies, eggs are much smaller in size than the caterpillar which is much smaller in size than the pupa which is much smaller in size than the actual butterfly once it has grown and morphed into its last stage – a butterfly. Looking at the unborn baby, you may consider growth when the doctors measure the baby every few weeks to see if it has grown or if it has increased in size and weight because they want to make sure the baby is healthy and they determine that by stating that the unborn child should be a certain weight, size and etc. by each stage of the trimester. You may consider the development of the unborn baby again in comparison to how other unborn babies weigh and look as well as how their heartbeats beat/sound and the growth of their body parts and organs at each trimester. The same way with babes in Christ. You may see their natural growth as far as them getting older and may seem to look wiser or dress more Christlike compared to the first day they walked in. You may see their growth when you hear them talk about the Word of God or see them reading the Word of God or studying the Word of God. You may witness their development by hearing them now quote scriptures verbatim versus needing to reference and look at their physical Bible. You may see development in their spiritual walk where they may be excelling much farther than they did on the first day they came into the House of God. You may see their psychological and mental development in gaining an understanding of God's Word and utilizing that Word to share with others in the correct context. At the same time, you may see development in them as they not only read God's Word, able to digest and regurgitate God's word properly and effectively while applying God's word in their life.

Whether it is a butterfly, an unborn baby or a babe in Christ, growth and development are significant. In order to see a butterfly, the female must lay the eggs, the caterpillar must eat and the development stages must take place. In order to see an actual unborn baby outside of the womb survive, there are certain growth and development patterns the mother must adhere to such as prenatal vitamins, doctor checkups, examinations, ultrasound, eating the right foods, being in a stress free environment and things of that nature. Now of course every pregnancy is different and some say they never had a prenatal vitamin in their life and their children turned out perfectly well. Again, the same way each of our spiritual growth and development are different, is the same way the comparison of the pregnancy is different. Lastly, lets review the babes in Christ. For their growth and development to take place, they must be willing. They must assemble themselves. They must submerge themselves into what it is to be Christlike by reading His word, gaining and understanding the knowledge of His Word and most importantly asking questions. Be present. Go to the weekly meetings. Go to Bible Study. Be present for the various services and learn. Seek the Lord and ask for a mentor to help lead you and guide you in your growth and development. For the butterfly to develop, it all starts with the female laying the eggs searching for the proper and safe environment. In order for the unborn baby to develop, it does start with decisions from the mother and those decisions can help or hinder the baby's growth and development. Lastly, in order for babes in Christ to develop, it all starts with their yes, being a willing vessel, being hungry and thirst after righteousness while lining up their cocoon and those that will surround them. They must know that what God has for them is for them while standing on their testimony.

The Adult Stage

Chapter 8

From Broken to Blessed

When the caterpillar reaches the final stage and becomes an adult which is the full butterfly, I'm sure it is relieved when it breaks through the chrysalis to reveal its new body for the world to see. No longer is it a roundish, ovalish-shaped, whitish-colored egg. No longer is it an ugly, hairy and weird-looking caterpillar. Instead, everyone marvels at the beautiful colors or beautiful color the caterpillar has now become. In this adult stage, the butterfly is famished and in search of food and a mate. Before it goes off in search of the two, it must give time for its new wings to work and get the blood flowing through its entire boy. Once that is complete, off it goes and the entire cycle repeats itself. It would not be unfitting to say the caterpillar went from what appeared to be a broken state to a blessed state due to its growth and development process.

With the unborn baby, it went through roughly 40 weeks of its nourishment, growth and development process and no longer looks like a small mass on a screen but instead has developed into a human being that weighs several pounds. The unborn baby went from a fetus (again an unrecognizable matter of mass) and blossomed into a fully developed, eight fingers, two thumbs and ten toes fully developed human being. It would not be unfitting to say that the unborn baby went from what appeared to be a broken and unrecognizable state to a blessed state due to its growth and development process.

Last but definitely not least, when looking over the babes in Christ, one is able to recognize not only the physical growth and development but the other natural and spiritual growths as well. It is hard to determine with babes in Christ how long the growth and development stages are. It varies for everyone and no matter how long a person has served the Lord, we are always ever-changing and ever-growing. As the Apostle Paul said, we have not obtained. We are still striving and reaching for the high calling in Christ Jesus. Even though we are ever-evolving in Christ, one should still be able to see development and growth. The same things that bothered you previously should be one step closer to not bothering you. Which each passing day, we strive to do better and better.

Striving to do better is a goal we want to accomplish in our journey and walk with Christ as well as our relationship with others. When we strive to do better, we try to not hold grudges. Many of us strive to do better. We think about the decisions that we did or didn't make and how we can improve our way of life if we find ourselves with a very similar or the same opportunity again. This is the process of the adult stage. As adults, sometimes, we get hurt. We get hurt mentally by family, friends, spouses, our children, our siblings and those who profess to love us as well as ministry, leadership, our employer, coworkers and including by those in the church. We sometimes get hurt emotionally and financially as well as physically. More times than not, we try and shake the dust off of our feet and continue on. We try not to let the situation or those involved wear us down. We try to see the brighter side and assure ourselves that the sun will come out tomorrow. We try our best to not pitch our tent in pity-party land but sometimes our emotions, thoughts and our hurt get the best of us. With all that we have suffered through in life and our journey with Christ, we feel like we are on this never-ending roller-coaster – sometimes just waiting for the high to come back and for the lows to end. We go through seasons of change and difficulties and we feel like it is not for the better but the worst. BUT ! I am here to tell you that it will not always be like this. It's a process and we must trust God through this process of developing, making and molding us. Just like the butterfly is transformed from the "ugly" caterpillar stage, it is still beautiful in God's eyes and able to be used. I am here to tell you and to encourage you that it does not matter what others do or say to you. God is still God! He sits high and He looks low. He reins on the just as well as the unjust. Don't allow anyone to take the beautiful colors that God has used to make and create you to twist and contort you into something or someone unrecognizable. Who would have known that the beautiful and confident woman that is writing this section of this book was teased and taunted by her blood-related family, was called all kinds of names that I couldn't even spell at that young age and was made to feel like I was a fifth-class citizen (if such one exists)? There were times that I felt that I was adopted and didn't belong in the family that I was in. I felt that surely God made a mistake by allowing my grandmom, my mom and I to reside in the family that we were in. There had to be a mistake. We didn't look like the rest of our family, we didn't talk like the rest of our family, we didn't act like the rest of our family and truth be told, they made us believe at times that we were not family. Some things they said and did to us I wouldn't wish upon my worst enemy. But God! He allowed the things I went through to not break me but to help me be a bridge over troubled water for others. In the process of loving me through those seasons, God allowed me to heal and forgive those who trespassed against me. He allowed me to forgive those who tried to break my spirit. He allowed my heart to be soft and pray for them and showed me that I was not on a path of bitterness but I was on that path to being blessed. We all go through a process and eventually evolve – like the stages a butterfly goes through – to then blossom into this amazing butterfly: a vessel that God can use for His glory with an amazing testimony to help heal others and teach them too to learn how to forgive along their journey.

Yes, at times, we think we're not worthy, we feel like we get fed garbage and at times it seems lonely but God has a beautiful plan written especially for us. We may have to crawl on our belly sometimes but soon we will learn how to fly with grace and beauty toward our purpose and the path God has destined for us.

Just as the butterfly is released from its last stage, God does the same with us and releases us into the world. We spread our wings telling any and everyone our testimony all while talking about the goodness of God and spreading the Good News that includes freedom in Christ; for which we are not bitter for what we went through and are no longer broken but instead we are blessed.

About The Author
Joshua De Sousa

Joshua A. De Sousa is a minister, conference speaker, youth leader, ghostwriter, and writing coach, using every opportunity possible to glorify God with his written and spoken words. He is a native of New Jersey and has been preaching the Gospel since the age of 14 years old. Joshua's online ministry presence, "De Sousa Declares Devotionals", consists of his daily social media posts, a blog, YouTube videos, and a newly launched podcast.

As a writing coach, he provides prayerful assistance, wisdom, and strategy for hundreds through his annual online writing conference, “Supernatural Scribes”. Joshua has four other books in different Christian genres. The first two from 2020 are a devotional and sermon collection entitled *Dew Drops of Destiny Vol. 1: A Plethora of Prayers, Promises, and Proclamations,* and a Christian superhero novel entitled *The Kairos Knight Scroll I: The Remnant.* The other two are a Christian writing manual called *AUTHOR-ity: The Scribe Guide,* and a memoir entitled *The Breakthrough of the Black Sheep.*

Other Works By The Author Joshua De Sousa

- AUTHOR-ITY
- Dew Drops Of Destiny Volume 1
- The Kairos Knight – Scroll 1: The Remnant
- Breakthrough of the Black Sheep
- The Identity of an Intercessor
- The Purity Pursuit
- The Faith to Forgive

Sousa Scribal Solutions

About The Author
Kimberly Stratton

Pastor Kimberly Stratton is originally from Delaware but currently resides in the sunny state of Florida. She takes care of her amazing Mom and together the Mother-Daughter Team love serving the Lord in any capacity. Usually, that service is in their home church called Church At The Well located in Sanford, FL where Pastor Kim is one of four Pastors and her Mom serves as the Greeter. The other capacity involves serving the Veterans, the elderly, the homeless and less fortunate through the 501c3 community outreach ministry called International H.O.P.E. Inc.. The HOPE stands for Helping Overcome Poverty Everywhere locally in Pennsylvania, Florida and other states as well as internationally including the Dominican Republic, Thailand and Africa.

Over the course of time with serving the Lord, Pastor Kim has worn many hats in the House of God and regardless of the number of hats she has and will wear in ministry, she takes great pride in being a servant first. Pastor Stratton says that she sees her life as Lee Williams said, "I'm just a nobody trying to tell everybody, about somebody, who can save anybody". That somebody is Jesus. If she can help somebody along the way, then her living will not be in vain. With that being said, Pastor Kim's life belief is that *"change always starts with ordinary people doing extraordinary things for the greater good."*

Other Works By The Author Kimberly Stratton

- A Voice For The Silent Ones
- It's StoryTime Vol. I ~ Coloring Book
- It's StoryTime ~ The Journey
- It's StoryTime ~ The Journey Continues
- It's StoryTime ~ The Journey Never Ends
- Yet Will I Serve Him ~ autobiography
- Yet Will I Serve Him part 2 ~ autobiography

To Contact the Publishing Co

Are you interested in writing or having your work (book, manuscript, poetry, how-to-do, autobiography/biography, etc.) published? Or maybe you are looking for consultation services? Then reach out to the publishing company. We provide an array of consulting and publishing services.

The Crown And Cross Consulting And Publishing Co LLC
Attention: Kimberly Stratton – CEO and Founder
PO Box 952607
Lake Mary, FL 32795
Email: thecrownandcrosspublishingco@outlook.com

THE CROWN AND CROSS CONSULTING AND PUBLISHING COMPANY, LLC

KIMBERLY STRATTON
FOUNDER AND CEO

NEW SERVICE ADDED: GHOSTWRITING

OUR NEWEST ADDITION TO THE C&C FAMILY, JOSHUA DE SOUSA, IS A MINISTER, AUTHOR, WRITING COACH, AND GHOSTWRITER WITH OVER 10 YEARS OF EXPERIENCE! HE SPECIALIZES IN MEMOIRS, AUTOBIOGRAPHIES, BIBLE TEACHING, DEVOTIONALS, AND EVEN FICTION! WITH HIS ASSISTANCE IN TYPING YOUR BOOK, YOU COULD HAVE A FULL MANUSCRIPT IN THE NEXT 3-6 MONTHS!

WORK WITH US TODAY BY EMAILING
THECROWNANDCROSSPUBLISHINGCO@OUTLOOK.COM
OR SOUSASCRIBALSOLUTIONS@GMAIL.COM

Notes

www.ingramcontent.com/pod-product-compliance
Lightning Source LLC
LaVergne TN
LVHW050538100826
845148LV00002B/605
* 9 7 9 8 9 8 5 3 7 5 4 6 6 *